CW01211606

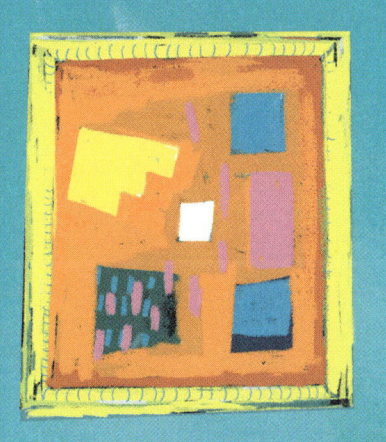

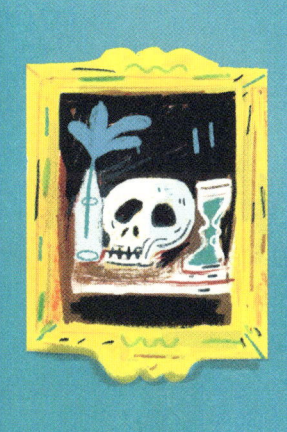

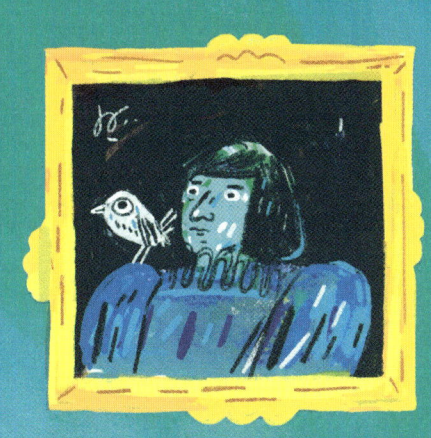

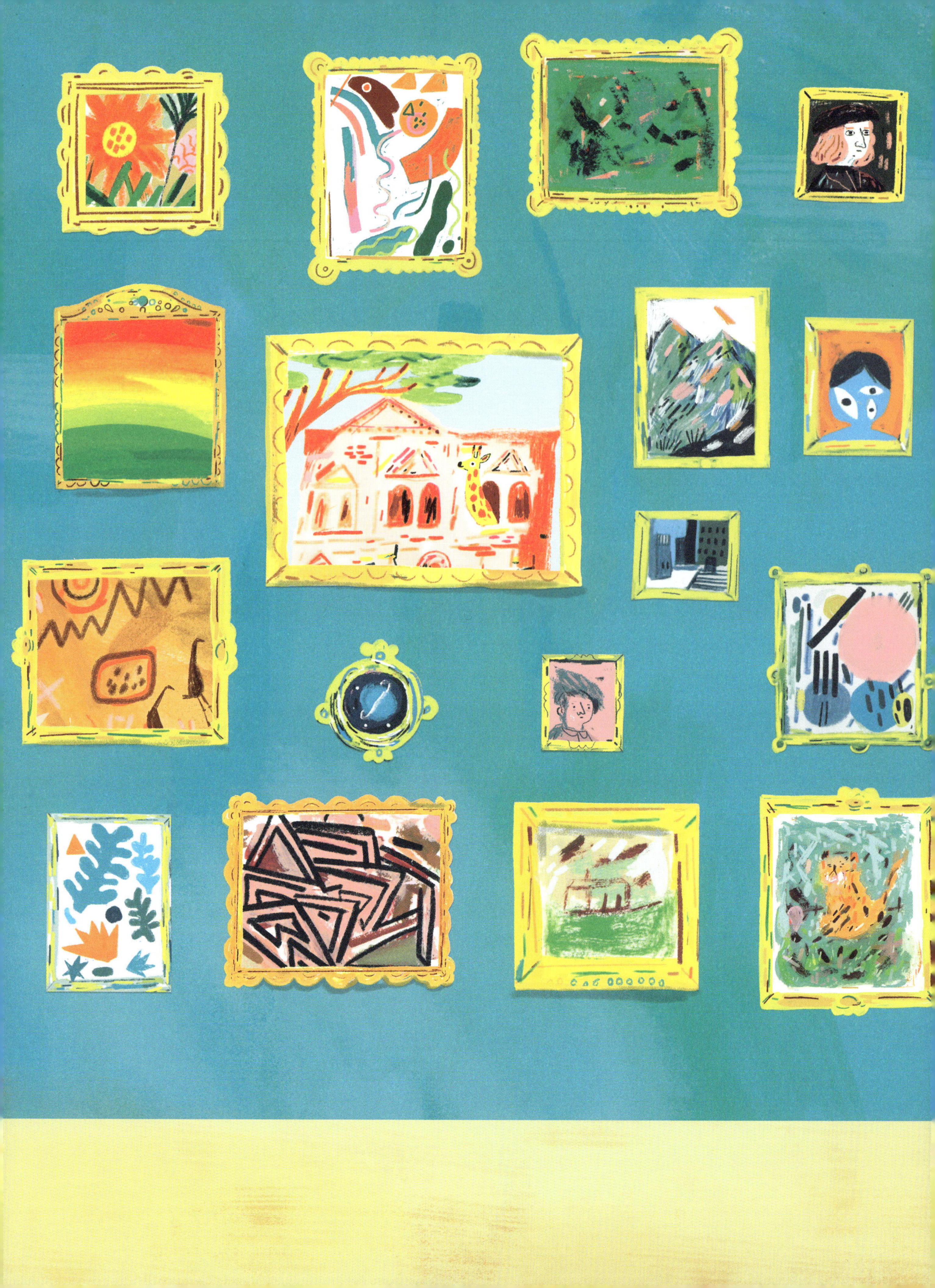

ART IS EVERYWHERE

For Mittens and Rosa — E.C.
For the wonderful dreamers in my life, and
Summer Town maker — L.B.

BIG PICTURE PRESS

First published in the UK in 2022 by Big Picture Press,
an imprint of Bonnier Books UK,
4th Floor, Victoria House
Bloomsbury Square, London WX18 4DA
Owned by Bonnier Books
Sveavägen 56, Stockholm, Sweden
www.bonnierbooks.co.uk

Design copyright © 2022 by Big Picture Press
Illustration copyright © 2022 by Liv Bargman
Text copyright © 2022 by Ellie Chan

1 3 5 7 9 10 8 6 4 2

All rights reserved

ISBN 978-1-78741-910-0

This book was typeset in Mr Dodo and GFY Brutus
The illustrations were created using crayons,
watercolour, felt tips, pencil and coloured digitally

Edited by Isobel Boston and Lydia Watson
Designed by Winsome d'Abreu
Production by Nick Read
Picture researcher: Ruth Smith

Printed in Latvia

Ellie Chan

Liv Bargman

ART IS EVERYWHERE

BPP

This is Keith,
a world-renowned art historian.
Keith also happens to be an ostrich.

This is my thinking hat.
Rather good,
isn't it.

'Art history' is quite a grand term. If you like, when you use it, you can put on your imaginary thinking hat. Art historians like Keith study works of art and explore how their meanings have changed throughout history.

This is Keith's esteemed research assistant, Marmaduke.

SO WHAT *IS* ART?

Art has been around for hundreds of thousands of years. Every time someone made a piece of art, they did it to tell the world something — from expressing their beliefs and feelings, to capturing a moment in time. Keith's favourite thing about art is that everyone sees it slightly differently. Every time someone looks at a piece of art, it gets a brand new meaning.

Art can be made out of pencil or paint, clay or stone, or needle and thread — almost anything at all! Art is all around us and it's used for all sorts of things — and it's not always to look beautiful!

Many people in the past said that ostriches can't be art historians, Keith sure showed them!

Perhaps you'd like to know a bit more about where Keith is from. Often, though, where you are from isn't the most interesting thing about you. The most interesting thing about you is where you are GOING.

Art has the power to transport you anywhere – from the streets of Venice to outer space!

The **Streets of Venice**

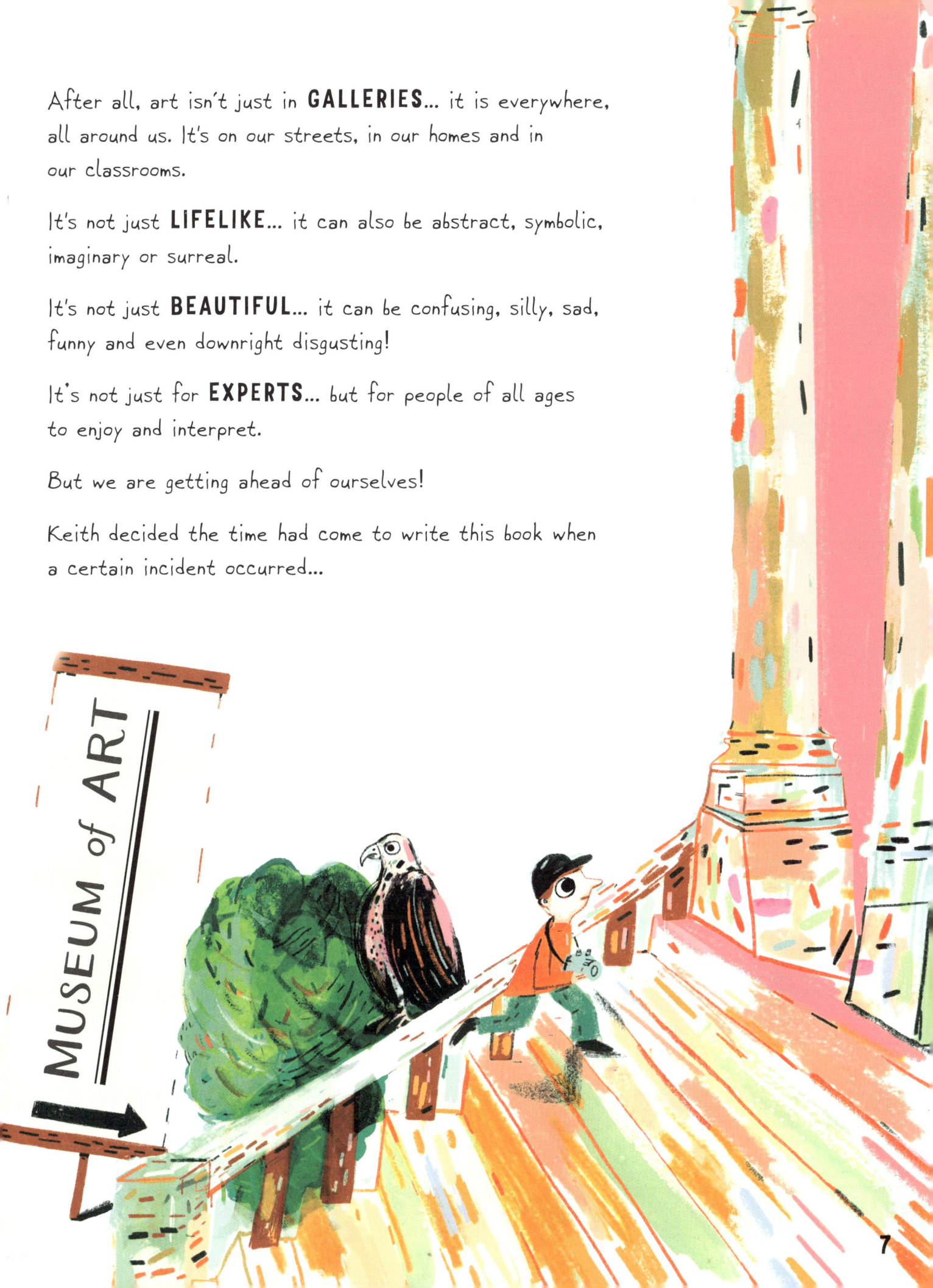

After all, art isn't just in **GALLERIES**... it is everywhere, all around us. It's on our streets, in our homes and in our classrooms.

It's not just **LIFELIKE**... it can also be abstract, symbolic, imaginary or surreal.

It's not just **BEAUTIFUL**... it can be confusing, silly, sad, funny and even downright disgusting!

It's not just for **EXPERTS**... but for people of all ages to enjoy and interpret.

But we are getting ahead of ourselves!

Keith decided the time had come to write this book when a certain incident occurred...

MUSEUM of ART

The **INCIDENT** was this.

Keith was in a big gallery somewhere, looking at the artwork on display. There were a lot of other people doing the same thing. I mean A LOT. With some pieces of art, you even had to wait your turn to look! And then Keith noticed something.

There were hundreds, there were THOUSANDS of beautiful, gorgeous, sumptuous pieces of art. Art as far as the eye could see! But the people visiting the gallery were only looking at the art that they were told to look at, or at the pieces that they recognised. They took a photograph, and then they quickly moved on.

Keith tried to get the crowd's attention to show them the many other marvellous paintings, sculptures, pots and textiles, but they ignored her. This made Keith rather angry.

'This isn't what art is about,' Keith thought as she left the gallery.

The really exciting thing about art isn't crowding into a room to look at one famous painting. The exciting thing about art is the way it makes you feel and the things it can show you.

Art is a language, just like English and Swahili and اَلْعَرَبِيَّة (Arabic) and 粵語 (Cantonese). It can tell you stories through its lines, patterns and colours. The trick is learning how to recognise what art is trying to show you!

"Art is everywhere and for everyone to enjoy. And I'm going to prove it," said Keith to Marmaduke.

You can find art in all sorts of places – it can be over your head and under your feet. In fact, one of the earliest forms of art we know of was painted in caves 40,000 years ago by early humans! You can still see their paintings of animals and patterns in caves today.

One very special thing about these paintings is the way the artists have managed to draw the animals with just a few lines – showing the suggestion of the animal's shape. Even thousands of years later, artists are still trying to do the same thing. What kind of shapes can you make with one line?

WHY DO WE MAKE ART?

Artists have many different motivations when they're creating their work. Some artists are trying to capture a particular moment in time, but others might be trying to create something that is beautiful or controversial — even if it means bending the truth!

When we're looking at a piece of art, we should never forget that we're seeing the world through the maker's eyes. Art is *always* the product of the artist's imagination — no matter how realistic it looks! Can you see the different ways Keith has painted Marmaduke here?

REALISM started in the 17th century. Inspired by the invention of telescopes and microscopes, artists tried to depict things as accurately as possible.

IMPRESSIONIST artists from the 1860s believed the best way to create art was by capturing the 'impression' of what things looked like to them.

ABSTRACT ART started in the 19th century. It is made up of lines, shapes and colours. Although the art has no subject, the artist is still trying to show a specific emotion.

SURREALISM began in the 1920s. This movement was all about making dreamlike imagery. Some of it is really, really weird!

13

In the 17th century, the artist Canaletto moved whole buildings around to try to make the scenes in his paintings as appealing as possible. His paintings look realistic, but they are actually imagined!

Can you see how Canaletto has changed the skyline of Venice in this painting? That's right – he's moved the church and the bell tower next to the bridge!

BRUSH STROKES

Artists use lots of different sorts of marks when creating their work. This is to make you think hard about how to look at it.

These marks provide more than just an outline of the artwork – they're used to create a particular effect.

For instance, when artists use certain brush strokes on landscape paintings, it brings the scene to life! You can almost feel the wind whistling through the trees or see the light reflecting on the water.

By using certain brush strokes, the artist Mary Cassatt wants to make you think about how something feels or moves.

In the below painting, the artist J. M. W. Turner has used brush strokes to capture the drama of this storm! What kind of brush strokes can you use in your own paintings?

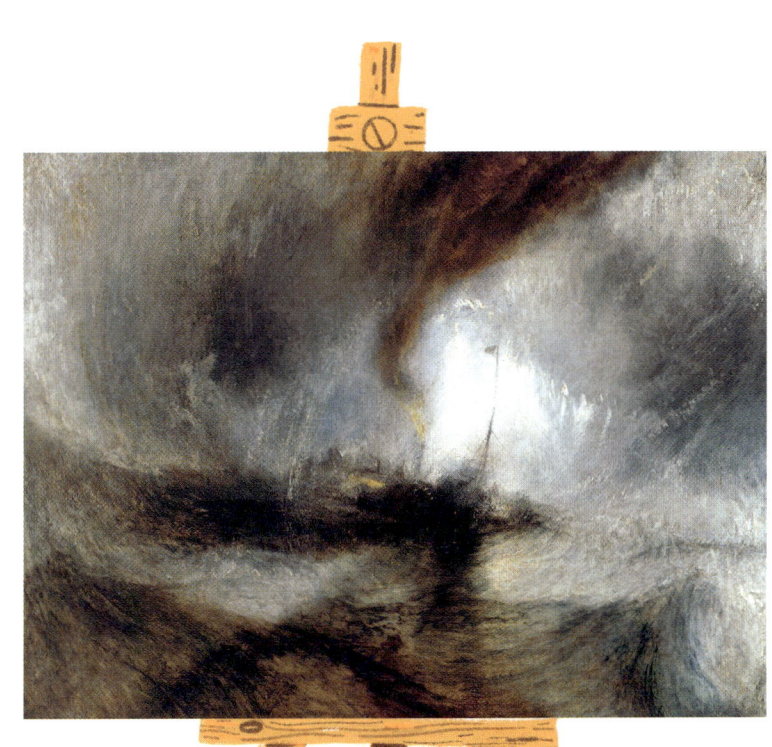

17

This lady was painted over 500 years ago! Today we call her the Mona Lisa.

She looks familiar — like she would be perfectly at home hanging on your bedroom wall or taped to the fridge. She looks like she knows you...

Part of the reason for this, is that her eyes and mouth have been painted with soft brush strokes so she looks a bit *fuzzy*. This makes her look like she's about to break out into a smile, or like she's just stopped laughing.

Using these kinds of soft brush strokes gives the impression of movement — just like when Keith's trying to take a photograph of Marmaduke and he just WON'T! SIT! STILL!

18

This self-portrait by Nicholas Hilliard was made in the 16th century and it's so small it can fit in the palm of your hand! Keith has made the picture much bigger here so you can see all of the tiny details. By layering lots and lots of paint over the man's clothes, the artist has made them stand out from rest of the painting. As you look at the portrait, the light catches the raised brush strokes and make the man look like he's about to move!

PATTERNS IN ART

A pattern is a repeated design and it's used in all sorts of art.

Artists use pattern for lots of different reasons — from drawing attention to a specific detail to adding texture. Patterns can make you think about how hard or how soft something is, or how smooth or how knobbly it must feel.

Sometimes, if you're really lucky, you're allowed to touch the art to find out how it feels — but mostly you just have to imagine!

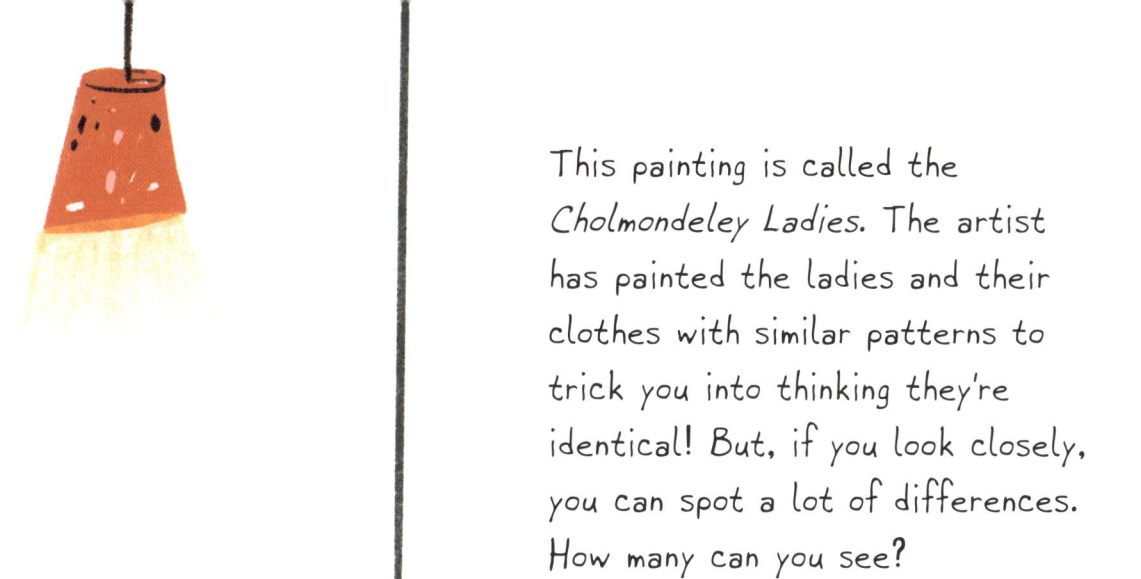

This painting is called the *Cholmondeley Ladies*. The artist has painted the ladies and their clothes with similar patterns to trick you into thinking they're identical! But, if you look closely, you can spot a lot of differences. How many can you see?

The same patterns have been used throughout history and across the world! Let's take a look at two of Keith's favourites.

This frilly leaf pattern is called an acanthus and the ancient Greeks used it to show off their most important buildings. The design is connected to a Greek myth. In the story, a nymph called Acantha insulted the god Apollo and he turned her into an acanthus plant! Because of the myth, the plant was associated with rebirth and immortality.

Look at the way the acanthus leaves reach up into the sky, making the columns look taller!

Spiral patterns can be found on all sorts of art – from paintings to textiles. In the past, spirals were seen as a symbol of the gods and it was even believed they could help you to communicate with them! Marmaduke loves the way spirals lead your eyes round and round...

The French artist Henri Matisse made this painting by arranging different pieces of coloured paper together. Does the pattern of shapes remind you of anything? It's supposed to look like a snail!

23

WHAT ARE GESTURES?

Artists use lots of clever techniques to get across the meaning or story behind their artwork. 'Gestures' are small, subtle movements – usually of the hand, head or body – that trick you into viewing an artwork in a particular way. Gestures can be tiny or HUGE. The way an artwork is arranged can reveal a lot about what the artist is trying to show you!

This sculpture by Barbara Hepworth is called *Mother and Child*. The artist has carved the sculpture out of smooth limestone and arranged the figures closely together so it looks like an embrace. Can you see how the mother looks like she is supporting her child?

The subtle curves and shapes of this *Dancing Stone* sculpture gives the impression of movement. Artist Lilly Henry has carved the sculpture in this way to make it look like the figure is dancing!

FANCY DRESS THIS WAY

Sometimes gestures are much more obvious! Look at these two pieces of clothing. They're beautiful things to wear, but they also make the wearer look BIG and STRONG and take up lots of space.

These pieces of clothing are made out of very different materials – metal and fine fabric – but the way that the designers have shaped them has made them look big and impressive!

The dress and the armour were both designed to make a statement – they say: 'I am powerful'.

Keith likes to think that her feathers can be used in the same way. When she is feeling a bit more informal, they are nice and sleek, but she likes to make them extra BIG and FLUFFED-UP when she's trying to be noticed – like now!

THE POWER OF COLOUR

Colour is one of the most expressive tools that an artist can use.

Each shade tells a story and has the power to evoke a different emotion. Today, you can buy tubes of paint in just about any colour you can imagine, but 300 years ago artists had to mix up their own colours! They would crush plants, stones and even insects into a powder and mix it with egg or oil.
Colours were chosen with care and had very specific meanings.

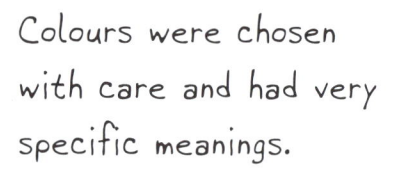

Pink was once a mighty colour. It was associated with battles and soldiers.

Yellow was associated with power and royalty in ancient China. Even today, people decorate their homes with yellow colours to bring good fortune!

Green has been associated with all sorts of things throughout history – from the natural world to aliens!

The way colours are used can create lots of different effects. The colours in the above painting clash and look like they are arguing with each other. This makes the painting look very dramatic!

29

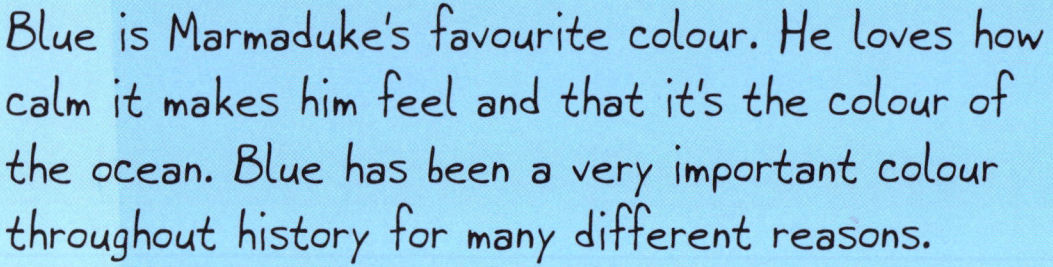

Blue is Marmaduke's favourite colour. He loves how calm it makes him feel and that it's the colour of the ocean. Blue has been a very important colour throughout history for many different reasons.

In 1000 BCE, ancient Britons painted their bodies with a blue dye to make them look extra scary when they went into battle! Back then, blue was a FIERCE colour. The warriors made the blue dye by boiling a special plant called woad.

WOAD CLASSES

In the past, blue was used to show that something was special or important. Part of the reason for this was because it was so expensive to make!

Between the 14th and 18th centuries, artists used a shade of blue called ultramarine in their art. Ultramarine was made out of crushed up gemstones called lapis lazuli – so artists were literally painting with jewels! Because of this, the colour was usually reserved for high members of society.

You can make ultramarine quite easily out of chemicals today, but artists still like to use it. In 1960, the artist Yves Klein used it to invent his own shade of blue called 'International Yves Klein Blue'. Klein made it the focus of his art because he thought it was such a powerful colour!

WHAT IS A SYMBOL?

A symbol is a solid, recognisable thing — like an object or plant or animal — that stands for a message, or something that's difficult for an artist to show. For example, doves have been used to represent peace and stars have been used to represent infinity.

Symbols are supposed to be recognisable. They're a bit like when a person walks past you on the street and tips their hat to say hello! Artists have used the same symbols in their work for centuries.

Look closely at this painting – what do you see? This is a portrait of Queen Elizabeth I of England and it was painted during a time when people loved to cram lots and lots of symbols into their paintings. You can join their meanings together like jigsaw pieces to work out the story behind the artwork.

Pearls are often seen in Elizabeth's portraits. She wore them to symbolise her purity and her wealth.

Elizabeth's cloak is really wacky! It is covered with hundreds of tiny eyes, mouths and ears to show how she is all-seeing and all-hearing.

Elizabeth was 68 years old when this painting was made, but she looks really young! Elizabeth liked to appear otherworldly in her portraits, like a fairy or a goddess. Her face is used as a symbol – it was another way of showing her power to her subjects.

33

Rainbows have always captured human imaginations. The rainbow has had many different meanings throughout history – from peace and hope to pride and diversity.

In Greek mythology, the goddess Iris was the messenger of the gods and she sent messages by rainbow! Medieval artists really liked this idea and depicted angels with rainbow wings. Rainbows were seen as a sign of hope and a promise of protection.

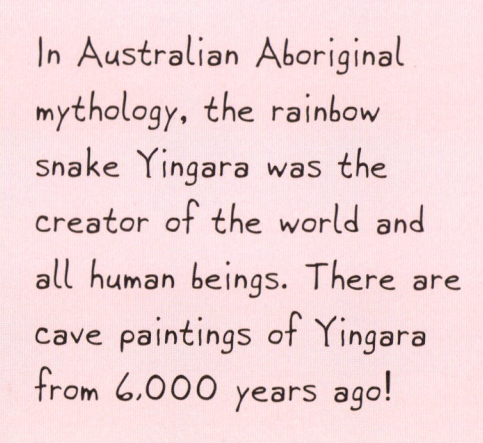

In Australian Aboriginal mythology, the rainbow snake Yingara was the creator of the world and all human beings. There are cave paintings of Yingara from 6,000 years ago!

In this painting, the artist J. M. W. Turner uses a rainbow to create a peaceful, idyllic atmosphere. The rainbow unifies the composition — that means it joins the separate parts together. Turner is celebrating the beauty of the castle with this elaborate flourish!

Keith loves that symbols have the power to bring people together. What does the rainbow mean to you?

ART CAN BE ANYTHING!

Sometimes, people think that art can only be paintings or sculptures. But actually, there isn't a right or wrong way of making art. It can be anything that a person creates to express themselves!

It can be **DRAWN**...

It can be **SHAPED**...

It can be **PRINTED**...

It can be **SEWN**...

It can be **KNITTED**...

It can be designed on a **COMPUTER**...

It can be made out of **FLOWERS**...

...or **BRICKS**

...or **GLASS**. Anything at all!

38

This piece of art was made out of gunpowder and fireworks!

Gunpowder was invented in China in the 9th century and throughout history it has been used as a way to destroy things. The artist, Cai Guo-Qiang, wanted to show that gunpowder could be used to make something beautiful — and that destroying things can create new lovely things!

39

Some art can even be made out of things you find. Art can be created out of all sorts of ordinary objects – things from your classroom or even on your street!

The piece below is called *Fountain* and it started out as a practical joke! In 1917, artist Marcel Duchamp turned a urinal upside down, signed it with a fake name and submitted it to an exhibition in New York. The piece was rejected because the judges said a toilet was "not a proper work of art" – even though everyone who paid the exhibition fee was supposed to have their work shown!

Some people thought *Fountain* was too silly, but others argued that being silly doesn't stop things from being art! Today, artists can use ordinary objects in many pieces of art.

Art can be inspired by all sorts of things. If you are walking around, playing in the park, or even just sitting in a chair you don't normally sit in, something can spark an idea.

It can be really fun to share your ideas with a friend. Marmaduke has some really crazy ideas sometimes, but he makes Keith see the world slightly differently! He is probably Keith's *favourite* artist.

41

It had been a very long day and Keith and Marmaduke were tired.

They arrived at a much smaller gallery and decided to go inside. There was all sorts of different art on display – Keith looked around happily at all of the sculptures, paintings, pots and patterns.

42

But next to a particularly interesting sculpture, a group of children were looking through the window and pointing at something on the beach below the gallery. "LOOK!" they cried.

Someone was making a BEAUTIFUL piece of art — right there on the beach. It was marvellous.

43

Keith and Marmaduke followed the children outside to get a closer look.

They watched as the children helped each other build the sculpture — shaping the sand and decorating it with beautiful shells, patterns and bright colours.

Keith smiled as she watched the children laughing and playing together.
'Yes', she thought. 'This is what art is all about.'

And so, at last, Keith took off her thinking hat and settled down with Marmaduke to watch the sunset.

IMAGE CREDITS

This book is filled with all sorts of art — some of it might be familiar and some of it you might never have seen before. Keith wanted make sure you were looking at *everything* in this book, not just the art which you thought you should be looking at! You can find out more about the art in this book below:

Wassily Kandinsky, *Improvisation No. 30 (Cannons)*, 1913, Alamy/Heritage Image Partnership Ltd
Page 5

Canaletto Capriccio, *The Rialto Bridge and The Church of S. Giorgio Maggiore*, circa 1750, Alamy/Vidimages
Page 14

Mary Cassatt, *Little Girl in a Blue Armchair*, 1878, photo courtesy National Gallery of Art, Washington, Collection of Mr. and Mrs. Paul Mellon
Page 16

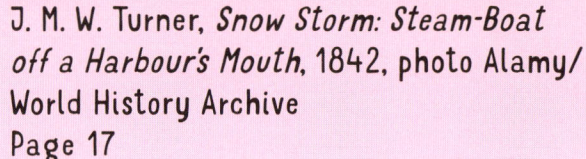

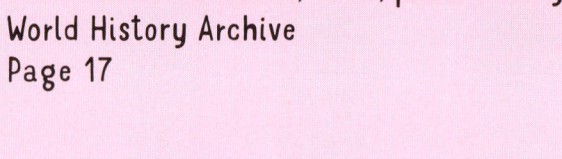

J. M. W. Turner, *Snow Storm: Steam-Boat off a Harbour's Mouth*, 1842, photo Alamy/World History Archive
Page 17

Leonardo da Vinci, *Mona Lisa*, 1503, photo Alamy/GL Archive
Page 18

Nicolas Hilliard, *Self-portrait*, 1577, photo Bridgeman Images
Page 19

Unknown Artist, *The Cholmondeley Ladies*, circa 1600-10, photo Alamy/Album
Pages 20-21

Henri Matisse, *The Snail*, 1953;
© Succession H. Matisse/ DACS 2022, photo Tate
Page 23

Barbara Hepworth, *Mother and Child*, 1934 (Ancaster stone), Barbara Hepworth © Bowness, photo Bridgeman Images/© The Hepworth Wakefield
Page 24

Lilly Henry, *Dancing Stone III*, 2017, www.lillyhenrysculpture.com
(contact: info@lillyhenrysculpture.com)
photo Lilly Henry
Page 25

David Allan, *Sir William Hamilton*, 1775, photo Alamy/The Picture Art Collection
Page 28

Claude Monet, *Bridge over a Pond of Water Lilies*, 1899, photo Alamy/Everett Collection Historical
Page 29

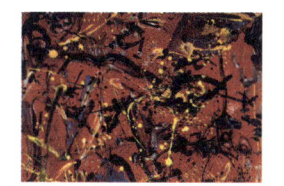

Jackson Pollock, *Red Composition*, 1946, © The Pollock-Krasner Foundation ARS, NY and DACS, London 2022, photo Alamy/Artepics
Page 29

47

Unknown Artist, *Emperor Daoguang (1782-1850)*, 19th Century, photo Highshines, Public domain, via Wikimedia Commons
Page 29

Sandro Botticelli, *The Virgin and Child (The Madonna of the Book)*, 1480, photo Alamy/classicpaintings
Page 31

Yves Klein, *Large Blue Anthropometry*, circa 1960, © Succession Yves Klein c/o ADAGP, Paris and DACS, London 2022, photo: Alamy/agefotostock
Page 31

Healy, George Peter Alexander, *Portrait of Elizabeth I of England (1533-1603), in ballet costume as Iris (Rainbow Portrait)* circa 1600-1602, photo Shakko, Public domain, via Wikimedia Common
Page 33

The Rainbow Serpent (Aboriginal Rock Painting), photo Alamy/mauritius images GmbH
Page 34

Jan van Eyck, *The Annunciation*, circa 1434/1436, photo courtesy National Gallery of Art, Washington, Andrew W. Mellon Collection
Page 34

J. M. W. Turner, *Arundel Castle on the River Arun with a Rainbow*, circa 1824-5, photo Alamy/The Picture Art Collection
Page 35

Cai Guo-Qiang, Poppy Series: Hallucination No. 1, 2015, Gunpowder on canvas 183 x 608cm, Private Collection, photo: Lydia Ohl, courtesy Cai Studio
Page 39

Marcel Duchamp, *Fountain*, 1917 (Replica) © Association Marcel Duchamp / ADAGP, Paris and DACS, London 2022, photo Alamy/IanDagnall Computing
Page 40

48

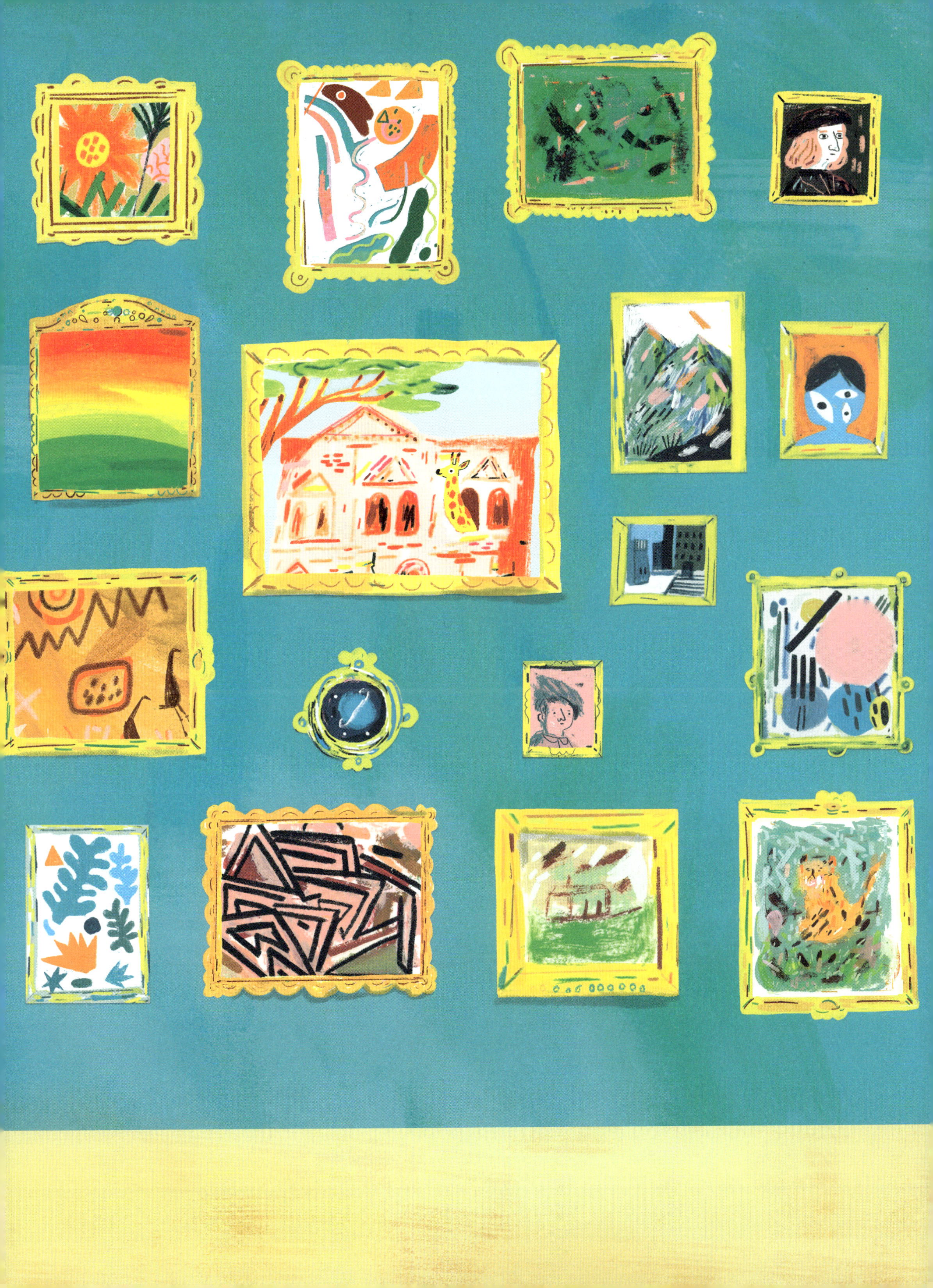

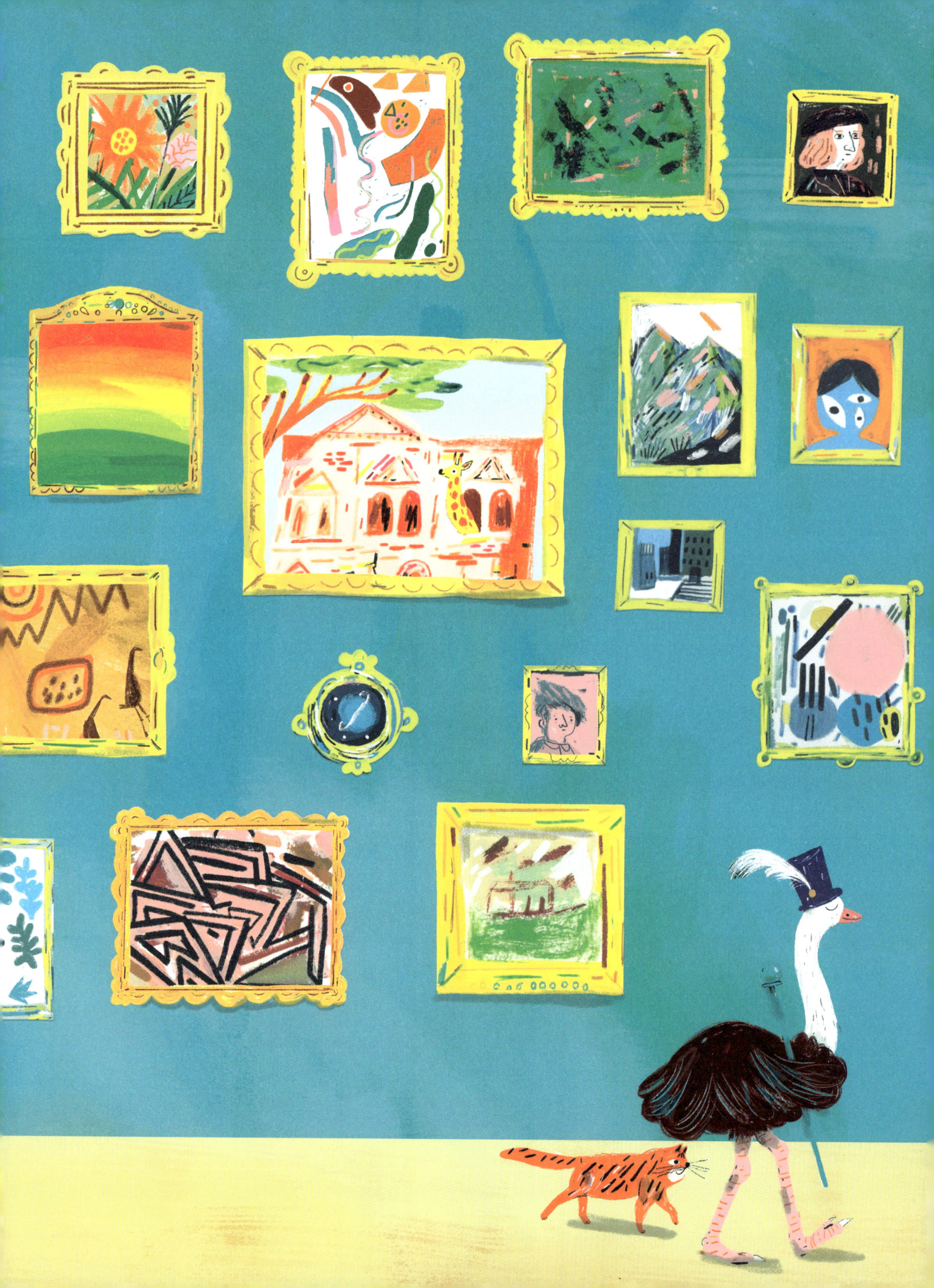